A Trafford Childhood

Frances Lennon

Willow
PUBLISHING

Best Wishes
Frances Lennon

Christmas 2000

Willow Publishing

Willow Cottage, 36 Moss Lane,
Timperley, Altrincham,
Cheshire, WA15 6SZ

ISBN 0 946361 15 0

Printed by The Commercial
Centre Ltd., Clowes Street,
Hollinwood, Oldham.

Down our way

At dusk the Lamp Lighter came down our way, turning people into shapes and shadows as he criss-crossed down our street, lighting up the gas mantles with his long stick. The Lamp Lighter wore a flat cap at a jaunty angle, the Knocker-up wore a pot hat, and he tapped on the windows with his long stick at 5 am every morning, barring Sundays. Sometimes they changed jobs, sometimes they met each other, and sometimes one of them did both jobs, and then he just changed his hat.

Everything and everyone took on a new dimension at twilight. I stood at the corner of our entry watching the workers make their way home from the British Westing House, Trafford Park. The vendors were on their last rounds; 'arry 'ead sold his penny oranges for a farthing on Friday night, at twilight, on pay night.

It was the early twenties; the war that was to end all wars was over. The dead had been mourned and were still mourned. Widows and orphans looked with hope to the Government for a new low rent house. The refugee lodgers we had tried to sort out their lives; the wounded tried to pick up the threads of theirs.

It was about this time that I started to draw in caricature and silhouette, using my school nib and my Dad's ink. Dad, who knew what I was about, did a funny walk for me under the gas light and his workmates Charlie Murphy, Jack Collins and Mr Mc'Loughlin did likewise. They made me laugh, for here were live, moving, dancing, humorous figures I could not wait to draw and remember forever.

Contents

Firing the Chimney

After the coal strike, due to all the burning of rubbish, we would require a sweep from time to time. The sweep was the most comical of my silhouettes, but Mother thought he was a might too dear at half a crown a sweep, so she fired the chimney herself, then we only had him at Christmas time and Spring cleaning. Mother would light a piece of paper and push it up the flue on a windy day.

It was fun to watch the sparks shooting out of the chimney and big pieces of charred Sunday Chronicle flying like kites in the sky, bursting into thousands of particles of dust and soot which made us cough enough to be given a piece of treacle toffee. We kept a sharp look out for the Bobby, for this was an illegal practice. We gave fair warning by singing 'Big feet, big feet, cover the street also smell so sweet'. Then up the flue went the ever ready bucket of water, with a warning from Mother, 'Don't tell your Father until he's had his tea'.

Sniffing the Tar

There was a sure cure for the Whooping cough down our way. Neighbours took us in groups wherever there was a 'diggin'. Our Mothers would take turns in collecting the children without the 'Whoops' so that they could pick up the germ from their friends. 'Getting it over with' they called this. Icky the Watchman and Bobby Larkin kept a weather eye on us and a blind one if necessary.

We liked the smell of the tar burning on the coke, we had to open our mouths wide and breathe in deeply. We liked the home made treacle toffee we got for a treat afterwards and the block of camphor slung around our necks on a piece of ribbon. We got used to the very hot water and mustard our feet were plunged into in the tin bath. Bringin' th'eat from th'ead this was called.

We did not like the thick black spanish, cod liver oil and Parishes food we were dosed with, a big spoonful of all fours, our noses held whilst powdered allum was blown down our throats. We hated the Goose grease spread on brown paper and slapped on our chests, then rasins soaked in senna pods, a good dose of this. The Old Tom beer with the red hot poker stirred in it was a treat and the tonic of beetroot soaked in stout was great but we had to be twelve to get some of that, only the girls, for rosy cheeks.

It was a case of kill or cure down our way or our Dads would be paying Doctor Hartherns collector two bob a week for a long time. The smell of the camphor, the Fishermen's Friend cough drops, the Firey Jack, the Goose grease and the results of the senna pods would have to be smelt to be believed in our classroom, no wonder the teachers were bad tempered from time to time.

Cock-a-Doodle-Do

We all kept chickens or rabbits in our back yards. We kept the cock in ours; he was my brother Wilf's pet. He fed him every morning with bread and jam and shredded wheat. Came the day, when the landlord, the nice landlord, who gave us Cadbury's Neapolitan milk chocolate so that we would open the door quickly to him when he called for his rent on a Monday, one day, said that we would have to get rid of all fowl in our back-yards or the rent would go up a lot.

Dad hummed and ahhed for a long time about killing the cock, so Mother got a local man to do it instead, for half a crown. Mother wanted value for money, she could have bought a cock for less, so she plucked it and made a pillow with the feathers, then she put it in the cooking pot.

I told Wilf that his Cock-a-doodle-do was in the cooking pot, and he was sick, then disappeared for a long time. I was in trouble. Mother said my tongue would get me hung one day; Dad said I should have thought before I spoke.

Dad could not eat the cock, he said it was tough; Mother said it was delicious, pretending that she had never tasted anything so good before, and I lost my appetite.

The Guild Hall

At the Guild Hall Mr. Birtles taught us to dance. One two, three, one two three, turn to your partners and bow. Gertrude Gresty was the star turn and later her displays at the pageant were the pride of Trafford. Here in the Guild Hall we had our Christmas parties with a Christmas tree that reached the ceiling and a present for everyone.

We paraded in this hall, hoping that one of us would be chosen for a leading part in the Pageant which took place every summer to help the hospitals. I never did become Rose Queen. When I had the chance to be Joan of Arc, Mother was afraid in case I fell off Peggy – Porrellis' ice cream cart horse. Joan of Arc always rode her in the processions and her back was as broad as a platform. 'Frances is accident prone' said Mother, and that was that. They made a jester of me instead, but what fun it was to dance and tumble before her Majesty the Rose Queen, on the green in Longford Park. In the Guild Hall, Ada Greenwood taught my sister Mollie and her friends to make paper roses to dress the lorries.

The Pageant

Down the Lane, Edge Lane, Rule Britania ruled, not only the waves but the generous hearts of the people of Trafford. They filled the collecting boxes to overflowing with gifts for the hospitals, in the hope of one day building a new one at Davyhulme Park. Stretford War Memorial hospital was the one we loved to help. How badly they needed our gifts, how hard the little families worked to put on this show, with so much enthusiasm and team spirit. Our Mothers made the costumes, Dads built up the floats and decorated the lorries and horses which were loaned by local farmers. The woodwork and other skills came in very handy for the display. We met behind the gas works in Ashover Street, or behind the Old Cock Hotel, Poplar Grove Road, or at Trafford Bar, to dress the lorries, according to where that year's Rose Queen was to be chosen.

One year our Dads got the bright idea of a lorry displaying Faith, Hope and Charity. There was a strike on at the time and they were all out of work, so they expressed their feelings in this way. They made a cross, painted it gold, then a heart and an anchor, and by these stood three beautiful young girls, my sister Mollie, being one of them. They wore their hair long, down to the waist, one dark haired, one fair, one auburn, and had white gowns crossed with golden sashes. How wonderful, thought I, to be beautiful, to be twelve, better still to ride on a lorry.

Alas, it seemed I was never meant to ride in style, so I danced the minuet with a group all the way down Chester Road and Edge Lane to the green in Longford Park. I wore white pantaloons, an embroidered jacket, lace and frills, and a wig that would not stay put. My partner danced daintily beside me in crinoline gown, frowning at me for treading on her toes, whilst I tried in vain to put straight my wig.

The Good Lady Spinster

Miss Carroll spent all day every day praying, in church and out of it. People called her odd, but she was much misunderstood and she proved to be very clever, although some days, she said, she was 'flummoxed' (confused). Children made fun of her old-fashioned clothes, and I must confess we often mimicked her. Some children were afraid of her, others loved her, but we called on our way home from school to talk to her, for she always had time for us. Time is the best gift anyone can give to a child, and Miss Carroll was generous.

I was curious like her cats, but her tabbies frightened me; they hid behind numerous plants staring at me with green eyes in the shadows of the gas light which she kept turned down very low.

I was ordered by my Mother to go and see if poor Miss Carroll wanted any errands fetching, before the last lamp was lit – I had to be indoors by then. I sat on her prickly sofa, surrounded by nick-nacks and wat-nots, and bits of old lace and crochet, whilst she tried to find her money inside a purse under a cushion.

She would tell me how lucky I was to be growing up in this day and age, because of the things I would see, but she would not, like the switches on the wall which would flood the whole room with light at the touch of a button. Streets would light up when one man touched a switch. But what about my Lamp Lighter and my pictures, I would think. She read my thoughts, 'You will still have your pictures, my lovely, but in a different way, you will write your name on them'. Then she continued 'you will not pick the black-berries on the Moss, your pinny all stained and torn; my, oh, my, you've brought some for me. They will build houses on top of houses on the Moss, reaching to the sky', she said, and they did just that on the Moss Vale where I once picked the blackberries. 'Very soon,' said Miss Carroll 'you will hear beautiful music coming all the way from London Town, you will hear the King speak, and our Charming Prince of Wales, who will never wear a crown. You will hear all this from a tiny box with no wires at all called a wireless; a cats whisker will make it all happen. Film stars will talk and sing in a box in your own parlour,' she said. 'Why will our Prince Charming never wear the Crown?' I asked. 'Because if he falls off his horse once more he will have no head to crown,' was the answer. I told my friends all of this as they sat on the wall waiting for me. They thought I had made it up about the cats whisker, they thought I made everything up. When I tried to convince them they said she was mad and I was madder for taking it all in. She was a kind lady and she gave me a penny and an orange for doing her errands.

Mrs. Never Sleeps

It would be impossible to mention all the wonderful shops and shop keepers in the Trafford of the twenties and early thirties, but everyone knew a 'Mrs. Never Sleeps,' as she was called, later becoming the household word of 'Mrs. Never Shuts'. The new shop keepers this last twenty years are still called Mrs. Never Shuts.

Mrs. Never Sleeps had a daughter Florrie 'ardbread. She was nicknamed 'ardbread because the bread was stale on a Bank holiday Monday, as it had been delivered on the Friday, but we were glad of it if the home baking had run out over the weekend, with extra visitors and, come what may, Monday was wash day not baking day. Tuesday was ironing day, Wednesday was baking day, Thursday sewing day, Friday cleaning day, Saturday shopping day and Sunday was a day of rest and peace and prayer. However, Mrs. Never Sleep never shut and she kept a really good shop, a little gold mine in fact. Bobby Larkin, who was always on the beat, knew her well, but she just paid the fine. We would buy anything, any time, on tick until Friday night, pay night, with good polite service and a lot of local gossip thrown in.

We had to brave the wild cats, of course, who lived in the cellar and had a nasty habit of flying up the chimney and over our heads just as we were about to enter the shop. Mostly they sat on the roof peering down at the customers and screeching cat calls, until Florrie 'ardbread satisfied their hunger with tit-bits which she threw down the cellar steps. Then, squealing meows, they jumped down the chimney and were quiet while Florrie sliced streaky bacon with a sharp knife.

Mrs. Never Sleep sold absolutely everything – everlasting bars, sweets called green peas, lamb chops and new potatoes, humbugs, gob stoppers, Tom Thumb drops, kahli as well as babies' dummies, thick twist tobacco, hardwear and margarine, (maggie-ann) sold in two pound blocks, and best butter patted into quarter pound pieces which we bought in case we had a visitor or Grandma came to tea. There were large blocks of cooking salt, fine tooth combs and senna pods; cakes and minerals side-by-side with novels by Ethel M. Dell and Ruby Ayres, chamber pots, fresh fruit, spices and pickles. The pungent smells coming from Mrs. Never Sleeps mingled with the smell of fish, chips and scallops from the other corner shop at the end of the street. It is a wonder that Mrs. Never Sleeps did not sell fish and chips too.

The Bazaar

We had fun with our neighbours the Roberts and the Watsons. The Bazaar in the Roberts girls' back-yard was really something. Besides brooches and sequins, beads buttons and ribbons found in various sewing machine drawers were sold as well as ten buttons for a farthing. They all found their way back home or into other sewing machine drawers in the next street.

The boys wound up His Masters Voice records on the green horn gramophone for background music. The records were 'Maggie', 'My Angeline', 'Oh, oh Antonio', 'Daisy, Daisy, give me your answer do', and the 'Sailors' Hornpipe' if it was cracked, as we could only have the cracked records to play with. The best ones were kept for Sunday afternoon to listen to with Father. We also had a back-yard May Queen, dressed up in old lace curtains and framed with a hoop decorated with paper roses.

Aggie 'olland's concerts were something else. No-one could produce plays like her. Aggie would give us a nice part to play if we gave her some props. There were plenty to be found in Grandma's old black trunk. The tam o'shanta Auntie Pollie wore when she married her soldier was blue velvet with a curled feather and it gave Cinderella's Prince more charm. The best play Aggie ever produced was the 'Sheik of Araby, his 'luv' belongs to me'. The beach towels were in full display on a red-haired Valentino who bent down on one knee to the glamourous Aggie who was decked out in every bauble and bead that could be found in her Mother's sewing box.

Mr. Perrelli sold us the best ice cream, Peggy his cart horse gave us the manure for our back-yard gardens. Peggy was big, wide, white, gentle and beautiful. Mr. Perrelli let us stroke her if business was good. 'I must be quick with my shovel and get that fresh manure before red-haired Johnnie beats me to it', I would think. I needed it for my sunflowers and sweet peas.

The Milliners and Other Shops

The Misses Cronell come to mind as I think about Easter bonnets, they were artists in millinery. Their bonnets were trimmed with forget-me-nots and lace. They were renowned for their wedding hats, even funeral hats were a joy to behold and lightened the step of many a widow.

There was a Pawn brokers called a Pop shop, where best suits went in on a Monday and were redeemed on a Saturday to be pressed ready for Church on Sunday. This shop was on Chester Road, at the corner of Edge Lane near the Hand Laundry where Dad had his white collars starched stiff.

Penningtons of Stretford was the place for prams and bikes; for sportswear and rain gear you could not beat Fitzpatricks. We had a secondhand furniture shop on Chester Road near Hollinsworth the Grocer and Wine merchant. Kings Street fascinated me – and the strong smells, the tea shop, the gossips, the flirting between boys and girls. The market, then near Lacy Street, was also a meeting place for young and old.

A look in at Green's toy shop in Gorse Hill was a must at Christmas time. Mr. Green was so very severe, twirling his waxed moustache whenever he saw our noses pressed against his clean window panes. Mrs. Green, so round and jolly, brought us inside and asked us what we would like for Christmas. 'Then go home and tell your Dads', she would advise. Mrs. Green had an eye to business in the toy shop near the Gorse Hill Hotel. It was in the same row as Winards the Butcher with the turkeys so fat and the geese hanging up outside in a row.

We would call on the Misses Lowe for some hair ribbons near the Post Office, then down Thomas Street we would go for some new bobble hats with socks to match from Mrs. Lewis, for one shilling and sixpence. Then we would pop in to Mrs. Cleaver's corner shop, not forgetting the cream from Mrs. Dooley's. Oh, but the shops were wonderful and the service so polite, except for Mr. Green. He told Mother that my nose would turn up forever if I did not stop pressing it against his clean window panes. The Ivor Novello profile was all the rage – one could never hope to be a film star if one's nose turned up, so I slept with a peg on mine that night but it made no difference. Then along came Clara Bow to the films and tip-tilted noses were fashionable.

May Day in Knutsford

Come Lassies and Lads, get leave of your Dads and away to the Maypole high', we sang as we crowned our back-yard May Queens and danced around the clothes prop decked out with paper roses, trying in our small way to match the charming celebrations of our neighbours in Knutsford, Cheshire. Even today May Day in Knutsford can take one back in time to a world of childlike innocence and peace that only the young and the young at heart can feel.

I remember my Dad's warm hand in mine, as he explained to me the meanings of the old customs, of Jack the Green, the little boy walking inside the pine tree, representing new birth and fertility. The Morris dancers around the Maypole, which at one time was cut from a birch tree and carried around the streets decorated with ribbons and flowers.

The old custom of the sanding is still held in Knutsford in the very early hours of the first day of May. The sandman sprinkles the coloured sand in front of the houses of the May Queen, Jack the Green, the Bride and Groom and any other members of the community by people who would wish them well. There were, and still are so many characters in this procession that it is impossible to name them all.

Besides the May Queen and her attendants there were Jesters, which no court could be without; there was the Muffin man, (one a penny, two a penny, hot cross buns), there was Cherry Ripe, Hansel and Gretal, the Witches and their cats, Alice in Wonderland and the Mad Hatter, Old Lace and Lavender girls, and the cow that jumped over the moon, to mention just a few. All this and much more enhanced by this charming old world village of Knutsford, the tiny town that derived its name from King Canute, Canutesford.

King Canute, it is alleged, when fording the river Lily, poured sand from his sandals at the feet of a newly married couple in the year 1017. This is what he wrote . . .
'Long may they live, Happy may they be,
Blest with contentment and from misfortune free.'

School Days

If at first I do not succeed then I must try, try, try again.' A hundred times I wrote these words and then some more. My teachers were not at all pleased with the little drawings they found around the edges of my exercise books. I had to start staying indoors at twilight, concentrating more to try to get my sums right. I did try working upstairs, but the Lamp Lighter came to light the lamp beneath my window and I began to daydream. Fairies flew around that lamp light, they bewitched me, they tantilized me, these sprites held me in their spell and my sums went all wrong. Six angry red crosses were placed by my six sums, I received a crack on the knuckles with the ruler and had to do a hundred more lines to try, try again. One day I saw a beautiful blue R on one of my six sums, so there was hope for me yet.

The Misses Griffins were very strict teachers; they took a lot of getting used to after the gentle Misses Cornthwaite.

Most teachers were spinsters in those days. The new headmistress and her sister swished the cane sharply and often across the legs or the palms of the hands. The boys tried to outwit them as they danced across the classroom swishing this long thin cane. The boys leaped like frogs over it, making sport of it, running the teachers around in circles. The rest of the class sat motionless and poker-faced trying to hold back the giggles in case it was their turn next. They turned out some good scholars from our school, I must admit, even the boy who wore the dunce's cap owned his own business when he grew up. We used to sing 'Pancake Tuesday is a very happy day if they don't give us a holiday we will all run away, where shall we run to, down Edge Lane, to meet Daddy Ball with his big fat cane.' Mr. Ball was the headmaster at Gorse Hill Council School and was a wellknown figure often to be seen walking down Edge Lane swinging his cane.

URMSTON
Long ago

The Five Bar Gate
Moss Vale

Jack Lane

Over the meadows
Down the lanes
Stop at the five bar gate
Make a promise
near Spite Row, where
lovers quarreled
long ago.

Higher Road
School

Gorsey Brow

The Empress Cinema

The Lord Nelson Hotel

Lovers Lane, Urmston

From Kings Street to Urmston Lane was Lovers Lane, for Urmston was the place for lovers and sweethearts to go walking. It was a little bit of country still left, for they were building fast. Glastonbury Road and Bradfield Road were still lanes, from Moss Vale to Gorsey Brow soon to be Humphrey Park Estate.

Gorsey Brow was where it is alleged that lovers quarrelled many years ago. Jack Lane to Ciss Lane was where we bought cut flowers and fresh chickens to take home to Mother as a peace offering if we were late. It was the early thirties, Bill was an apprentice in the Meter Department, Metropolitan Vickers Elec. Co. Ltd. If Bill and I and his dog Rover went out five minutes early we could beat Doris and her sweetheart and Emily and hers to the five bar gate on Moss Vale, or the fence on Barton Clough, where we fed the ponies with sugar lumps and talked of sweet nothings. Wilf and his sweetheart were off on a tandem around the Cheshire lanes. Our childhood days were over.

We enjoyed the meadows and the lanes, we watched the foundations being laid for dream houses, a sunshine house for fifteen pounds deposit and three hundred and fifty pounds mortgage. Here by the five bar gate we built our dreams, but alas, the rumoured depression came all too soon. The lads were out of work as soon as they could demand a man's wage. We could hear the rumblings of yet another war to end all wars.

Whit Week Walks

It is often said that it is always raining in Manchester. We never do 'chance it' without our umbrellas and there could always be a rainbow to look forward to afterwards. Whether there was rain, hail, shine or fog, Manchester and Salford Scholars turned out in splendour every day during the whole of Whit Week. With banners flying, dripping wet, they did not even notice that dye from the linen roses stained their pretty dresses, for this was Manchester and Salford's Profession of Faith.

Traffords schools were considered to be too far out of town to join in this magnificent parade. We were great spectators at the city walks. All denominations were represented, together with refugees and immigrants. Each denomination was strong in its own belief, complemented each in their strength and admired each other for it. Starting out from St. Ann's Square, led by the Bishop of Manchester, came the Cathedral choir, followed by school children from every parish in the city. Every poor child was 'rigged out' with new clothes given by various charitable organizations by voluntary workers.

On Whit Friday the R.C. Schools were led by the Bishop of Salford. Brass bands and Irish Pipers played as they had never played before. The sounds of rousing music echoed through the soot-grimed streets of our city, to the tunes of 'Land of Hope and Glory', 'God save the King', 'It's a long way to Tipperary' and 'Faith of our Fathers'. As the procession drew to its close, the Italian community appeared around the corner with a life-size statue of the Madonna carried by sturdy young men. It was laden with hundreds of fresh lilies. Like a thunderbolt came the clapping of thousands of people as they lined the streets. Children were lifted high on the shoulders of their Dads to witness the Profession of Faith and see the statue of the **Madonna in the Streets**.

Our Rainy Manchester

We loved a ride on an open-top tram car. There were many sights to be seen from this type of transport. We saw the very cheap shops down Stretford Road, the rows and rows of tiny terraced houses which seemed to be strung together in case they fell down, and neighbours sat huddled together on their front steps gossiping.

There were many charitable organisations in Manchester. The Manchester and Salford Methodist Mission did a great deal to relieve the sufferings of the poor. The Salvation Army saved many a family from starvation, and gave new life to many a down-and-out. Their tambourines played a clear and happy message and their cheerful hymns brought hope to all who heard them. Dad was a member of the S.V.P. Society, (St. Vincent de Paul Society), a group of men who volunteered to help the poor, the sick and the dying, in their spare time. Dad's work took him into the slums of Manchester.

Many a best frock of mine went missing when Dad was on a case. It seemed to me that there was always a little girl just my age who needed my frock more than me. It was the end of the world for me when my best red coat, my new white fur bonnet, my muff and my white kid boots all went missing. I was sent to church in my sister's hand-me-downs, several sizes too big for me. I was so bad tempered I could not say my prayers.

Dad took me for a ride on the open top tram car. From the top of the car I saw that there really were a lot of little girls just my age, and they had no shoes or socks at all, they were cold and dressed in rags and very dirty. I clutched tightly to my doll and vowed I would never feel so mean again. However I did understand how Dad felt when Mama gave away his best boots to a beggar at the door, for he had to go to church in his hob-nailed working boots. He cocked his well brushed pot hat on one side of his head, he wore his stiff white starched collar, a white silk scarf, his best suit, and then he shone up his working boots with spit and polish. With a wry grin, Dad said to me, 'Come on, Sunshine, we're in the fashion'.

Flixton

Flixton village could not be reached by tram car in the twenties as the tram lines were not laid so far out of town. We called it the other end of nowhere. Grand-da walked us all the way from Gorse Hill to Flixton, so we were glad of the benches along Church Road for a rest. Mother took us by train with a basket full of home made goodies for a picnic. We went from Trafford Park Station to Flixton Station. We watched the beautiful weddings and christenings at the old Parish Church of St. Michael, and with silent reverence we read the epitaphs on the old gravestones.

Close-by there were ponies to give sugar lumps to, cattle to watch and a pig farm, together with a village shop where we could buy humbugs or kahli and a tiny Post Office. The Jubilee tree was planted in Flixton in the year 1887 to celebrate the Golden Jubilee of Queen Victoria. Although this was before our time, there were other Royal occasions to enjoy with much flag waving and song and dance.

Another treat was a trip to Irlam by ferry boat, and crossing the penny toll bridge at the junction of the rivers Mersey and Irwell. In our childish imagination the river became an ocean, the sculled rowing boat a captured ship, and we were pirates carrying our treasures of kahli and humbugs to the boat-house for a refreshing drink.

'They pulled a good gill at the boat-house' said Grand-da. Our Grand-da was a great walker, he had two favourite walks, one was to Trafford Park Lake for a row in a boat, the other was to Bluebell Wood in Ackers Lane, Carrington. 'Only a mile,' said Grand-da, down the Mile Road. It was the longest mile I ever walked, trailing limp bluebells down the long hot road and then even further to the railway station.

Back home I would dream about the Bride of Shaw Hall and her knight in shining armour; and was it true about the White Ladye of Shaw Hall who, it is alleged, still haunts the pathway between Church and Hall called the Causeway, and was there really a secret passage? Flixton, the little village at the other end of nowhere, was full of surprises, and simple were our pleasures in the Trafford between the wars.

Flixton

A new front for the old Church Inn

The Legend of the Bride of Shaw Hall

The old Parish Church of St. Michael

The Jubilee Tree

Penny toll fare by ferry boat

Morris dancing in Flixton Village

STOP

Blackpool Works Week

The highlight of the year was a holiday in Blackpool. We went by train, the first week in July. Dad joined us for the last week of the month which was the British Westing House works week, and he brought with him his bonus. Bonus seemed to me to be spelled out in capital letters, because it held such promise. From the moment Mother dug out our buckets and spades from the cupboard under the stairs until we all trooped out to catch the train, for me it was one continuous trip to Katie's House, the outside white-washed lavatory. Mother got fed up with me, so did Tibby the cat; she insisted on following me on every trip.

Dad's wage as an Iron Turner in 'C' Engine Details, was approximately two pounds a week basic, but with overtime and bonus paid monthly, this paid for whosoever's turn it was for new shoes and the like. Mother was a good manager, she helped out with her knitted lace blouses which she sold to stout ladies and they did look glamourous when they draped the delicate silk over their ample bosoms. On very hard times she earned six shillings a week buttering teacakes and muffins at Mrs. Brooms tea shop on Trafford Park lakeside, so the month's holiday was provided for.

We stayed every year at Mrs. Nuttalls in Station Road, South Shore; she had a daughter Nora who was a joy. Nora sneaked chips up to our bedrooms at supper time, saying 'Don't tell Madam'. Mrs. Nuttall charged one shilling and sixpence a night for all of us. Everyone kept themselves, that is they bought their own food and kept it in a cupboard in the dining room. Mother told Nora what we would eat each day. During the first three weeks very little money was spent except on food which was bought fresh each day. Every day was a delight; the sand and the sea, the rain, the sunshine tanning us brown as berries. Punch and Judy and the Ventriloquist on the beach entertained us for a penny collection. We had great appetites.

My mouth watered as I watched Mother cut into the ridges of the famous Blackpool rolly-polly loaf, thickened with butter and treacle, a big wedge of Mothers cut-and-come-again cake which she always brought with us. We never ate bought cake and one would be ashamed to offer it to visitors. Tinned food was also beneath our dignity to eat but there was plenty of fresh food in the Blackpool shops, the shop keepers were old friends. On the first day we were weighed on the big brass machine on the golden mile. On the last day we were weighed again and had our photographs taken, then we went to the fair, after the one shilling and sixpence had been settled for; Dad had come with his bonus and all was well. Blackpool Westing House works week was the time to remember. This famous seaside in the North West of England still holds the same character but too many motor cars have taken away some of the charm of yesteryear.

The Charleston

Varied and wonderful were the shapes and shadows to be seen down our way and up the village. Fashion was slow to come to Trafford, people wore the same hats and coats for years. Our Mothers tried to bring us up-to-date by running up little print frocks on the sewing machine. The gingham was sixpence a yard, a bargain, so Mother bought yards of it in different colours. She kept the knitting needles flashing for jerseys and jumpers.

Down our way there were some flappers of course — young ladies of high fashion who shortened their skirts and dropped the waist-line to the hips. They wore garters, black ones with red roses on them, lisle stockings and pointed toes shoes, a cloche hat called a po hat, or a Nelly Kelly London style. A shingle hair cut or the bob or a marcel wave was a shilling well spent at the local hairdressers, and then they were all set to do the Charleston.

People doing the Charleston gave me the shapes I so loved to draw. I danced it all the time; everydone did. The old and the young, everyone's Grandmas, and Grandas were Masters of the Art. We danced every day, except Sundays, for Sunday was the special day when we did not even play a ball game or iron or sew, or fetch errands. It was a day of rest, of peace, of prayer, a family day, with a roast for dinner and an evening around the piano.

Edge Lane

Thinking of Edge Lane always brings to mind the blossoms, the sweethearts, the sunshine, and the romance. In this lane Stretford youth met Chorlton youth and many a date was planned, for dance or pictures. The pavement artist was there, brightening up the footpaths with his coloured chalk. This artist, wounded in the Great War, gave pleasure to his many admirers. Our Prince Charming of Wales and all the Royal Family were his favourite subjects. The pictures stayed on the pavement until the summer rain washed them away.

It was on the railway station in Edge Lane that we danced with excitement as the Knutsford train pulled in, for the annual outing to Tatton Park for the sports on Whit Saturday. Here we stood as teenagers with rusksacks on our backs, ready to start a ramble around Cheshire; here we took the train to Chester for a day on the river. We waved goodbye to our soldiers here and welcomed home our wounded.

Sundays

Every Sunday we attended early morning Mass at St. Annes Church, Stretford, and Sunday School in the afternoon. In the evening was the Benediction service, and afterwards the lads met the lassies, raising their new pot hats and sporting their plus-fours or Oxford bags. The girls would be giggling and pretending not to notice.

May and June brought the processions in and around this beautiful church. Many a best hat was worn with pride and the pictures to be seen as the congregation poured out of church and on to Chester Road were very colourful. The last of the hansom cabs arrived for old Mrs. Murphy and we all waited around to see her step into it.

40